German-American Genealogical Research
Monograph Number 14

EMIGRANTS FROM FELLBACH (BADEN-WUERTTEMBERG, GERMANY), 1735–1930

Clifford Neal Smith

CLEARFIELD

Reprint, March 1985   ±√
Reprint, October 1985   √
Reprint, March 1986   √
Reprint, May 1986   √
Reprint, September 1986   √
Reprint, November 1986   ± ∫
Reprint, February 1989   qz
Reprint, October 1991   qz
Reprint, January 1995   u
Reprint, January 1997   u

Originally published
McNeal, Arizona, 1984

Reprinted for
Clearfield Company by
Genealogical Publishing Co.
Baltimore, Maryland
2004, 2007

ISBN-13: 978-0-8063-5258-9
ISBN-10: 0-8063-5258-2

Made in the United States of America

INTRODUCTION

The following list of emigrants from the village of Fellbach, now almost absorbed by the city of Stuttgart, has been adapted from a German publication:

> Otto Conrad, Geschichte der Auswanderung aus Fellbach: Ein Beitrag zur Geschichte der schwaeb. Auswanderung, zugleich ein Kapitel aus der Familien- und Heimatsgeschichte Fellbachs (History of Emigration from Fellbach: A Contribution to the History of Swabian Emigration and a Chapter in the Family and Local History of Fellbach)(Fellbach-Stuttgart: Volksbund fuer das Deutschtum im Ausland, Landesverband Wuerttemberg, April 1934).

It is estimated that about 2,000 persons emigrated from the village of Fellbach between 1735 and 1930. Of this number, 1,421 were identified from village records and another 160 were added on the basis of oral information.[1] The sum total, then, is 1,581 identified emigrants. Herr Conrad reports that the records of the eighteenth century are incomplete and that many more individuals must have removed to northeastern Germany (Prussian Pomerania) than could be found in extant records; family members of emigrants to Prussia were never mentioned in the Fellbach records of the period. Herr Conrad also relates that

> "Some years ago (before 1934), according to information from the Fellbacher Rathaus, an invitation was received from Swabians in the Banat asking that representatives be sent to a celebration in the Banat honoring Fellbach settlers of 200 years ago. The invitation was signed by some of the descendants. However, the records in Fellbach did not list any of the settlers who went to the Banat."

The records used by Conrad in his compilation were as follows:

-- Kirchenbuecher (church registers) of Fellbach, volumes I-VI

-- Altes Seelenregister (Old Register of Souls)

-- Familienregister der Auswaertigen und Auswanderungsliste vom 1650-1888 (Family Register of Persons Abroad and Emigration Lists, 1650-1888) at the Fellbach Rathaus

-- Dr. Georg Leibbrandt, Die Auswanderung aus Schwaben nach Russland, 1816 bis 1823 (Emigration from Swabia to Russia, 1816-1823)

-- Dr. K. Stumpp, Die deutschen Kolonien im Schwarzmeergebiet (German Colonies in the Black Sea Region)

-- E. Eippinger, Beschreibung und Fuehrer von Fellbach (Description of and Guide to Fellbach)

According to AGRIGA,[2] the following records are available in the Staatsarchiv Ludwigsburg pertaining to emigration from Bezirk Cannstatt (or Bad Cannstatt), of which Fellbach was a subdivision. All these records are to be found under catalog number F 160, Canstatt:

-- Nr.097a: Lists of Passports issued, 1844-1923

-- Nr.099-: Supporting documents for passports issued, 1901-1923

-- Nr.118-: Losses of (Wuerttemberg) citizenship, 1887-1906

-- Nr.118a: Losses of (Wuerttemberg) citizenship, 1815-1865

-- Nr.118b: Losses of (Wuerttemberg) citizenship; lists of passports (Passkarten); lists of visas, 1866-1923

-- Nr.457-: Lists of Certificates of original domicile and of citizenship (with supporting documentation), 1889-1940

-- Nr.465-475: Lists of certificates of original domicile, 1887-1912

These records apparently were not consulted by Herr Conrad, but genealogical researchers may find them of value. Fellbach church registers apparently have not been microfilmed by the Genealogical Society of Utah (as of 1984) and presumably are to be found in Fellbach.

Historical Note. Herr Conrad observes that the emigrants were from families resident in Fellbach for generations and that most of these families were closely related to one another through intermarriages. The Sippe (extended family) Aldinger was closely related to the Lipp, Schaechterle, and Schnaithmann families. The Sippe Rebmann had connections with the Maile, Mergenthaler, and Hess families. Fellbach was, then, a typical peasant village, where families had been tied to the soil for centuries and rarely reached outside the immediate neighborhood for marriage partners.

There were several reasons for emigration, most prominently the lack of available agricultural land to accommodate an increasing population. The Remstal (Rems Valley) surrounding Fellbach is primarily a vineyard area, and it will be seen that a great many of the emigrants were Weingaertner (herein translated as winegrower).

There were other reasons for emigration--one being religious. The Remstal was scene of much religious separatism and sectarianism. In the sixteenth and seventeenth centuries the Widertaeufer (Baptists), known in America as the Mennonites and their splinter groups, had a considerable membership in the Valley. Even in the twentieth century Pietism is prominent in Fellbach's religious life. An example of the Separatist position is to be seen in an entry quoted in Leibbrandt, as follows:

> "In 1803 winegrower (Josua) Vaihinger of Fellbach, Oberamt Cannstatt, allowed his child to be christened at the urging of his wife, but declared that he held the sacrament of baptism to be of no importance--it being simply a superficial custom. [True baptism] is a matter of faith and confession [to be exercised by adult volition, not as a ritual of infancy]. Such belief was prevalent in other villages of the Remstal, notably in Schnaith, Winnenden, and Leonberg, and similarly in Markgroeningen."[3]

It will be noted that Josua Vaihinger and his family emigrated to Pennsylvania in May 1804. Conrad suggests that Vaihinger may have joined the Separatist movement of Johann Georg Rapp of Iptingen, Oberamt Maulsbronn, who founded colonies in Pennsylvania.

Napoleon was held to have been the Antichrist, and many emigrants moved eastward into Russia to await Christ's Second Coming. From 1807-1815 the Wuerttemberg government completely banned emigration because of the large numbers of would-be emigrants. The year 1816 was one of bad harvests and much hunger; it was thought to be yet another harbinger of the Second Coming.

Several secular events also caused Fellbacher residents to emigrate. One was the great increase in taxes during and after the Napoleonic Wars, in which Wuerttemberg was a participant. Another was the imposition of universal military conscription. Fellbach emigrants were attracted by the 1762 promises of the Russian Czarina Katherine II, reaffirmed by Czar Alexander in 1804, whereby tax and military exemptions and religious freedom were guaranteed to new settlers coming to Russia.

During the 1850s there was again a period of famine in Fellbach. Nine children of Johann Schmalzried, six children of Johann Jakob Schneithmann, five children of Gottlieb Friedrich Seibold, and four children of Georg Friedrich Volzer all starved to death. In these years there were many emigrants, some helped by community funds. A typical entry in community records reads as follows:

"August Friedrich Haeussermann, unmarried tailor, born 12 September 1821, emigrates to America with travel expenses paid by the community. He has been given the necessary funds and promises not to fight against King and Fatherland for the period of one year. He likewise renounces all rights of residency in this Community and citizenship [in the Kingdom of Wuerttemberg]."[4]

Links with America. Since the Fellbach records are so fragmentary for the eighteenth century, it is not possible to identify immigrants coming to America during that time period. However, in 1803-1805 one can link a number of Fellbacher emigrants with persons landing at Philadelphia, as reported in volume 2 of Ralph Beaver Strassburger's and William Hinke's Pennsylvania German Pioneers, cited as S&H in the list hereinafter. It is likely, however, that there were many Fellbacher immigrants before 1803; one strong clue is the fact that in the period 1803-1830 there were several apparently unaccompanied women journeying to America, no doubt to join relatives settled in the country before 1803. If the names of these settlers had been available in the Fellbach records, many of them would be identifiable in Strassburger's and Hinke's work.

1. The original list of 1,421 emigrants was first published in the local newspaper Fellbacher Tagblatt and readers were asked to report any names not included. This resulted in an additional 160 names, no doubt mainly the names of persons emigrating after 1870, who would still have been in living memory.

2. Clifford Neal Smith and Anna Piszczan-Czaja Smith, American Genealogical Resources in German Archives (Munich: Verlag Dokumentation, 1977; distributed in the United States by R. R. Bowker Co.).

3. Leibbrandt, op.cit., p. 32.

4. Gemeinde-Protokoll, volume 40, 1852/54, p. 145.

AICHINGER, Friederike Widow of carpenter; with 3 children	Brazil	1891
ALBER, Johann Friedrich, winegrower With family (2 children)	America	1880
ALDINGER, Anna Dorothea	America	1832
ALDINGER, Benjamin, winegrower With family (8 children)	Russia	1879
ALDINGER, Christian, shoemaker With family (4 children)	America	1881
ALDINGER, Christian Friedrich, winegrower	Russia	1831
ALDINGER, Christian Stephan	America	1804
ALDINGER, Christoph	America	1817
ALDINGER, Daniel	America	1830
ALDINGER, Elisabetha Margaretha	America	1830
ALDINGER, Elsa Daughter of the "Lindenhof" innkeeper	North America	1923-28
ALDINGER, Emile	America	1885
ALDINGER, Eugen (I) Son of the "Lindenhof" innkeeper	North America	1923-28
ALDINGER, Eugen (II)	America	1927
ALDINGER, Ferdinand (I), winegrower	America	1816
ALDINGER, Ferdinand (II), winegrower With family (3 children)	America	1816
ALDINGER, Gottlieb, winegrower	America	1854
ALDINGER, Gottlieb Friedrich (I)	America	1880
ALDINGER, Gottlieb Friedrich (II)	America	1887
ALDINGER, Gottlob, winegrower With family (3 children)	America	1853

ALDINGER, Gottlob Friedrich, winegrower With family (6 children)	America	1880
ALDINGER, Gottlob Friedrich (II)	America	1880
ALDINGER, Jakob Friedrich, winegrower	America	1857
ALDINGER, Johann	America	1817
ALDINGER, Johann Adam	America	1830
ALDINGER, Johann Christian, winegrower With family (3 children)	America	1817
ALDINGER, Johann Christoph, winegrower With family (6 children)	America	1817
ALDINGER, Johann Daniel, winegrower	America	1854
ALDINGER, Johann David	America	1832
ALDINGER, Johann Friedrich	America	1867
ALDINGER, Johann Georg, winegrower With family (4 children)	Brazil	1826
ALDINGER, Johann Georg (I)	Russia	1804
ALDINGER, Johann Georg, winegrower With family (6 children)	Russia	1829
ALDINGER, Johann Gottlieb, winegrower With family (2 children)	America	1878
ALDINGER, Johann Jakob	America	1866
ALDINGER, Karl (I)	Argentina	1921
ALDINGER, Karl Son of the Messner [acolyte]	North America	1927
ALDINGER, Karl Eugen	America	1909
ALDINGER, Karl Friedrich, missionary With family (3 children)	Switzerland	1870
ALDINGER, Karoline Philippine	America	1866
ALDINGER, Luise Katharina	America	1867

ALDINGER, Margaretha	America	1817
ALDINGER, Pauline Philippine	America	1867
ALDINGER, Peter, winegrower	America	1831
ALDINGER, Rudolf He died.	Argentina	1921

ALLMENDINGER, Johanna. *See* SCHNELLER, Johanna, nee ALLMENDINGER

BAEHRLE, Christian Jakob, winegrower With family (1 child)	America	1832
BAEHRLE, Friedrich, head waiter Returned to Germany in 1919	England	1899
BAEHRLE, Friedrich	New York	1879
BAEHRLE, Johann Christian	America	1832
BAEHRLE, Johann Daniel, winegrower With family (4 children)	America	1854
BAEHRLE, Johann Friedrich, soldier	Palestine	1872
BAEHRLE, Mattheus Friedrich, winegrower With family (4 children)	America	1820
BAEHRLE, Regina Katharina	America	1853

BAEHRLIN. *Alternative spelling for* BAEHRLE

BAEUERLE, David	America	1835
BAEUERLE, Johann Christian	America	1846
BAEUERLE, Johann Gottlieb	America	1846
BAEUERLE, Johann Jakob, winegrower With family (3 children)	America	1879
BAEUERLE, Johann Friedrike	America	1853
BAEUERLE, Johannes	America	1835
BAEUERLE, Karl Albert, blacksmith	Switzerland	1890

BAEUERLE, Marx	Prussian Pomerania	1801
BAEUERLE, Philippine Friedrike	America	1853
BAISCH, Adolf, tinsmith	America	1921
BAISCH, Ernst With family	America	1921
BAUERLE, Eugen, miller His wife and 2 children followed in 1933.	Philadelphia	1930
BAUMANN, Maria	Brooklyn	1926-28
BAUMANN, Wilhelm	New York	1926-28

BAUSCH, Georg
  With family (3 children); later returned to Germany; 1 son died
  in South America.
	South America	1924

BEBION, Michael, winegrower With family (6 children)	America	1849
BECK, Barbara, nee FREY With brother Philipp Frey and family	Russia	1875
BECK, Friedrich Married	America	1923
BECK, Georg Friedrich, winegrower	America	1840
BECK, Johann	America	1844
BECK, Katharina	America	1819
BENZ, Karl Gustav, tailor	Switzerland	1870
BERNHARD, Ella	Brazil	1933
BEURER, Gottlieb, winegrower With family (4 children)	America	1880

BEURER, Gottlieb Simon Son of the cabinetmaker	America	1816
BEURER, Johannes	America	1832
BEURER, Luise Dorothea	America	1854
BEURER, Michael, blacksmith	Egypt	?
BEURER, Philippine Friedrike	America	1853
BEURER, Simon Perhaps with family	Prussian Pomerania	1750
BIEDERMANN, Adolf	America	1923
BIEDERMANN, Albert Returned to Germany in 1929	Argentina	1923
BLIND, Karl Returned to Germany	North America	1921
BLOSS, Karl Wilhelm, glazier *See also* PLOSS	America	1854

BOLEG, Elisabetha Pauline
    Daughter of *Schultheiss* [village elder]
    [Note also surname BOLIG, BOLLICK in S&H 1:540 and 1:727]
	America	1850

BOLEG, Sophie Theresia Wilhelmine Daughter of *Schultheiss* [village elder]	America	1850
BREYER, Hermann Albert Son of the minister	America	1869
BRUEGEL, Johann Jakob, saddler With family (8 children)	America	1832
BRUEGEL, Karoline Heinrike	America	1836
BUBECK, Johann Husband died in America, wife returned to Germany; son in Brazil.	America	1924

BUBECK, Luise Christiane   America   1854
   [Note S&H 2:130 in which a Joseph BUBECK, with family, landed
   at Philadelphia in 1803 accompanied by Caspar LORENZ and family. LORENZ is listed in this monograph and it seems probable
   that Joseph BUBECK was also from Fellbach, although not mentioned in local records extracted.]

BUEHL, David	America	1816
BUEHL, Friedrich With family (4 children)	America	1817
BUERKLE, Anna Margaretha (I)	America	1817
BUERKLE, Anna Margaretha (II)	America	1832
BUERKLE, Christiane Dorothea	America	1817
BUERKLE, Gottlieb, winegrower With family (4 children)	America	1854
BUERKLE, Johann Peter With mother Magdalena BUERKLE	America	1851
BUERKLE, Johanna Luise Married woman with 2 children	America	1817
BUERKLE, Johannes	America	1817
BUERKLE, Joseph, winegrower With family (3 children)	America	1854
BUERKLE, Joseph Friedrich	England	?
BUERKLE, Karl Wilhelm, winegrower With family (1 child)	Russia	1879
BUERKLE, Magdalena With son Johann Peter BUERKLE	America	1851
BUERKLE, Wilhelm Friedrich, winegrower With family (4 children)	America	1880

BUERKLIN. *Alternative spelling for* BUERKLE

DANNER, Adolf Christian	America	1885

DEILE(N), ANNA DOROTHEA Daughter of winegrower	America	1831
DEILE(N), Michael, winegrower With family (3 children)	America	1852
DILL, Karl Johannes	America	1879
DINKELACKER, Gottlob Friedrich Brother of Wilhelm Heinrich and Karl Friedrich DINKELACKER	America	1865
DINKELACKER, Johann Friedrich	America	1817
DINKELACKER, Karl Friedrich Brother of Wilhelm Heinrich and Gottlob Friedrich DINKELACKER	America	1857
DINKELACKER, Wilhelm Heinrich Brother of Karl Friedrich and Gottlob Friedrich DINKELACKER	America	1853
DIPPING, Wilhelm	America	1880
EBENSPERGER, Auguste Luise Sister of Katharina Fridrike and Wilhelm Friedrich EBENSPERGER	America	1854
EBENSPERGER, Christian	America	1854
EBENSPERGER, Georg Friedrich	America	1854
EBENSPERGER, Johanna Margarethe Widow with 3 children	America	1882
EBENSPERGER, Karl Wilhelm	America	1883
EBENSPERGER, Karoline Sister of Luise EBENSPERGER and Katharina Barbara HAMMER	America	1856
EBENSPERGER, Katharina Barbara Wife of Georg HAMMER of Beutelsbach	Australia	1856
EBENSPERGER, Katharina Fridrike Sister of Auguste Luise and Wilhelm Friedrich EBENSPERGER	America	1854
EBENSPERGER, Luise	America	1853
EBENSPERGER, Marie Pauline	America	1882

8

EBENSPERGER, Thomas Friedrich Son of the baker	Hungary	1817
EBENSPERGER, Wilhelm Friedrich Brother of Auguste Luise and Katharina Fridrike EBENSPERGER	America	1854
EBINGER, Abraham	America	1830
EBINGER, Christiane With Simon EBINGER and mother	America	1854
EBINGER, Ernst	California	1923
EBINGER, Ernst Friedrich, missionary	Africa	1913
EBINGER, Georg Jakob, winegrower	Russia	1804
EBINGER, Johanna Friedrike Sister of Karoline EBINGER	Switzerland	1866
EBINGER, Johannes (I), winegrower With family (4 children)	America	1831
EBINGER, Johannes (II)	America	1836
EBINGER, Karl Friedrich, tailor	Switzerland	1850
EBINGER, Karoline Sister of Johanna Friedrike EBINGER	America	1866
EBINGER, Katharina, widow	America	1851
EBINGER, Simon With Christiane EBINGER and mother	America	1854
ECKARDT, Anna Maria (I)	America	1830
ECKARDT, Anna Maria (II)	America	1880
ECKARDT, David	America	1862
ECKARDT, Elise Barbara	America	1819
ECKARDT, Philipp Jakob	America	1851
ECKINGER, Luise	America	1817

ECKINGER, Maria Barbara	America	1822
ECKINGER, -- Widow of Joseph ECKINGER, with 6 children	America	1822
EHRLE, Karl With widowed mother	America	1923
EHRLE, -- With son Karl EHRLE; she returned to Germany.	America	1923
EKHARDT, Christian Brother of Jakob and Luise EKHARDT	America	1880
EKHARDT, Jakob Brother of Luise and Christian EKHARDT	America	1880
EKHARDT, Luise Sister of Christian and Jakob EKHARDT	America	1880
ELSAESSER, Ernst	America	1880
ELSAESSER, Heinrich Brother of Ernst, Hermann, and Wilhelm ELSAESSER	America	1880-83
ELSAESSER, Hermann (I) Brother of Ernst, Heinrich, and Wilhelm ELSAESSER	America	1880-83
ELSAESSER, Hermann (II)	America	1883
ELSAESSER, Johanna, widow Mother of Ernst, Heinrich, Hermann, and Wilhelm ELSAESSER	America	1880-83
ELSAESSER, Johannes (I), winegrower With family (7 children)	America	1819
ELSAESSER, Johannes (II), cooper Widower with 3 children	America	1853
ELSAESSER, Karl Heinrich	America	1882
ELSAESSER, Paul	Brazil	1922
ELSAESSER, Wilhelm Brother of Ernst, Heinrich, and Hermann ELSAESSER	America	1880-83

10

ENSSLIN, Ernst Christian Wilhelm	America	1863
ENSSLIN, Johannes, laborer With family (8 children)	America	1904?
ENSSLIN, Luise Pauline	America	1859

ERNST, Christian
  [Note S&H 2:156 which says he arrived at Philadelphia in
  1804 with Jacob HOFMEISTER, also listed in this monograph]
	America	1810

ERNST, Johann, winegrower	America	1870
ERNST, Johann Gottlob, butcher	America	1869
ERNST, Mattheus Friedrich, winegrower	America	1806
FAUSER, Gottlob Benjamin	America	1851
FAUSER, Johannes With wife	America	1852
FELGER, Georg Michael Son of winegrower	America	1843
FISCHER, Thomas	Prussian Poland	1803
FLAIG, Mattheus, weaver With family (1 child)	America	1849
FLEISCHMANN, Maria Returned to Germany	Holland	1924
FRECH, Jakob Friedrich	America	1860
FRECH, Johannes, winegrower With family (4 children)	America	1853
FRECH, Johann Georg, winegrower With family (? children)	America	1819

FRECH, Philipp Friedrich	America	1852
FREY, Georg Daniel, winegrower With family (5 children)	America	1852
FREY, Johann Friedrich, winegrower	America	1810
FREY, Johann Georg	Russia	1804
FREY, Johann Gottlob His son [unnamed] and family returned to Germany.	Russia	1879
FREY, Johann Michael	Russia	1804
FREY, Karl Brother of Karoline and Pauline FREY	North America	1892
FREY, Karl Bernhard, winegrower With sister Rosine Luise FREY	America	1855
FREY, Karoline Sister of Karl and Pauline FREY	North America	1892
FREY, Marx	Prussian Pomerania	1750
FREY, Pauline Sister of Karl and Karoline FREY	North America	1892
FREY, Philipp With family (4 children) and sister Mrs. Barbara BECK	Russia	1875
FREY, Rosine Luise With brother Karl Bernhard FREY	America	1855
FRITZ, Heinrich, businessman	Russia (Odessa)	1867
FRITZ, Johann Friedrich, carpenter	America	1879
FRITZ, O. His wife was Elsa KOHLER of Fellbach.	America	1923-24
GAUGER, Christian Friedrich, cabinetmaker With family (3 children)	America	1879

GEIGER, Christiane Friedrike	America	1849
GEIGER, Johann Wilhelm	America	1849
GEIGER, Luise Karoline	America	1853
GEIGER, Luise Margarete	America	1853
GLAUNER, Dorothea	America	1854
GLAUNER, Elisabeth Margarete	America	1853
GLAUNER, Friedrich David, winegrower With family (? children)	America	1816
GLAUNER, Jakob Friedrich	America	1803
GLAUNER, Mattheus (I) [See S&H 2:171]	America	1805
GLAUNER, Mattheus (II)	America	1819
GREINER, Wilhelmine Luise	Switzerland	1869
HAEFNER, Anna Magdalena	America	1832
HAEFNER, Maria Barbara	America	1832
HAEFNER, Michael, winegrower With family (1 child); emigrated to join his two oldest daughters	America	1857
HAEUSSERMANN, Agathe Jakobine	America	1837
HAEUSSERMANN, Anna Barbara, widow	America	1819
HAEUSSERMANN, August	America	1852
HAEUSSERMANN, Auguste	America	1852
HAEUSSERMANN, Caspar	America	1853
HAEUSSERMANN, Dorothea Friedrika	America	1846

HAEUSSERMANN, Euphrosine. *See* SEIBOLD, Euphrosine, nee HAEUS-
SERMANN

HAEUSSERMANN, Friedrike (I)	America	1817
HAEUSSERMANN, Friedrike (II)	America	1852
HAEUSSERMANN, Georg Jakob, shepherd With family (1 child)	America	1819
HAEUSSERMANN, Gottlieb	America	1818
HAEUSSERMANN, Gottlieb Friedrich, tailor With family (1 child)	America	1818
HAEUSSERMANN, Gottlob With family (2 children)	America	1880
HAEUSSERMANN, Gottlob Friedrich, winegrower Brother of Johann Georg HAEUSSERMANN	America	1852
HAEUSSERMANN, Jakobine With her child and 2 other children	America	1855
HAEUSSERMANN, Johann Adam, weaver With family (1 child)	America	1851
HAEUSSERMANN, Johann Adam (II), weaver With family (5 children)	America	1852
HAEUSSERMANN, Johann Georg Brother of Gottlob Friedrich HAEUSSERMANN	America	1852
HAEUSSERMANN, Johannes With family (4 children)	America	1880
HAEUSSERMANN, Karoline	America	1848
HAEUSSERMANN, Katharina Barbara	America	1832
HAEUSSERMANN, Luise	America	1848
HAEUSSERMANN, Maria Margarete	America	1830
HAEUSSERMANN, Michael	Prussian Pomerania	1750
HAEUSSERMANN, Pauline Friedrike	America	1880
HAEUSSERMANN, Pauline Philippine	America	1880

14

HAEUSSERMANN, Philipp Adam	America	1854
HAEUSSERMANN, Philipp Jakob	America	1854
HAGENMANN, Johanna Dorothea To join brother Paulus HAGENMANN in America	America	1854
HAGENMANN, Johann Georg Went to Schweidnitz, Silesia	Silesia [Germany]	1735
HAGENMANN, Johannes With family (? children)	America	1853
HAGENMANN, Magdalene Karoline To join brother Paulus HAGENMANN in America	America	1854
HAGENMANN, Paulus	America	1853
HAMMER, Katharina Barbara, nee EBENSPERGER Sister of Karolina and Luise EBENSPERGER	Australia	1856
HAMMER, Philipp David	America	1853
HARSCHER, Friedrike	Switzerland	1850
HARSCHER, Karoline	Switzerland	1850
HAUSLER, Johannes, winegrower With family (3 children)	America	1879
HAUSLER, Karl, iron worker [*Eisengiesser*]	America	1907
HAUSLER, Marie	North America	1923
HAUSLER, Mattheus Friedrich	America	1805
HAUSLER, -- [Three unnamed brothers and two sisters]	America	1853-54
HAUSMANN, Gottlob Friedrich	Switzerland	1840
HAUSMANN, Johann Michael	Switzerland	1830
HAUSMANN, Philipp Adam Brother of Philipp Jakob HAUSMANN	America	1854

HAUSMANN, Philipp Jakob Brother of Philipp Adam HAUSMANN	America	1854
HAUSSER, Beate Dorothea	America	1849
HAUSSER, Conrad Friedrich	America	1857
HAUSSER, Gottlob Benjamin Brother of Beate Dorothea and Johann Christian HAUSSER	America	1851
HAUSSER, Johann Christian Brother of Beate Dorothea and Gottlob Benjamin HAUSSER	America	1847
HAUSSER, Johannes, winegrower With family (? children)	America	1852
HAUSSER, Johannes (II), winegrower	Holland	1850
HAUSSER, Luise	Switzerland	1908
HAUSSER, Wilhelm Friedrich The thirteenth child in his family	America	1854
HEID, Friedrich David, winegrower	America	1847
HEID, Georg Friedrich	America	1830
HEID, Johannes	America	1835
HEID, Karoline With her child	Switzerland	1865
HEID, Marie Friedrike	America	1881
HEID, Wilhelm, winegrower	America	1865
HEIDINGER, Georg Friedrich, soapmaker With family (2 children)	Russia	1820
HERDTFELDER, Otto	Argentina	1924
HERZER, Johann Christoph, wagon master With family (6 children)	America	1830

16

HESS, Abraham Father of Jakob HESS	Russia	1882
HESS, Anna Maria, widow	America	1851
HESS, Balthes With family (4 children)	America	1887
HESS, Balthes Friedrich	America	1850
HESS, Elsa Sister of Emile, Klara, and Robert HESS	North America	1922-28
HESS, Elsa (II)	Geneva, Switzerland	1928
HESS, Emilie Sister of Elsa, Klara, and Robert HESS	North America	1922-28
HESS, Eugen, baker	Brazil	1923
HESS, Friedrich David	America	1857
HESS, Gottlieb Friedrich, baker With family (9 children)	America	1880
HESS, Gustav Now [1934?] in California	North America	1906
HESS, Heinrich	America	1906
HESS, Helene	St. Paul, USA	1923
HESS, Jakob With family (4 children)	Russia	1880
HESS, Jakob Friedrich	America	1836
HESS, Johanna Luise	Switzerland	1876
HESS, Johannes	America	1854
HESS, Josef Friedrich	England	?
HESS, Karl August	America	1853
HESS, Karl Christian	America	1854
HESS, Karl Wilhelm With family (1 child)	America	1883

HESS, Klara Sister of Elsa, Emilie, and Robert HESS	North America	1922-28
HESS, Paul	America	1894
HESS, Philipp (I), tailor With family (3 children)	America	1819
HESS, Philipp (II)	America	1906
HESS, Philipp Adam With family (4 children)	America	1888

HESS, Robert
  Brother of Elsa, Emilie, and Klara HESS; first emigrated to
  Holland, then to North America
	North America	1924

HESS, Wilhelm	America	1865
HESS, Wilhelmine, nurse [*Pflegerin*] Returned to Germany	China	1924
HEUSSER, Johann Friedrich [Possibly the Friedrich HAUSER in S&H 2:171]	America	1805
HEYDT, Emilie	America	1921
HEYDT, Fritz, mason	America	1906
HIRZEL, Johann Philipp	America	1836
HOEFER, Karl August	America	1870
HOEFER, Karl Heinrich	America	1870
HOEFER, Karoline	America	1870
HOELDERLIN, Anna Maria	Switzerland	?
HOESCH, Gottfried, winegrower	America	1850
HOESCH, Karl Wilhelm, cabinetmaker With family (4 children)	America	1883
HOESCH, Wilhelm Gottlob	America	1887

HOESCH, Wilhelm Heinrich	America	1872
HOFER, Adolf	France	1863
HOFMEISTER, Albert Heinrich	America	1906
HOFMEISTER, Balthes Friedrich Brother of Johannes HOFMEISTER	America	1865
HOFMEISTER, Balthes Friedrich (II) Winegrower; with family (4 children)	America	1866
HOFMEISTER, Christian Brother of Johann HOFMEISTER	America	1818
HOFMEISTER, Christoph Friedrich With family (4 children)	America	1854
HOFMEISTER, Emilie Sister of Eugen HOFMEISTER	North America	1923-28
HOFMEISTER, Eugen Brother of Emilie HOFMEISTER	North America	1923-28
HOFMEISTER, Gabriel With wife	America	1818
HOFMEISTER, Georg Friedrich, winegrower With family (4 children)	America	1817
HOFMEISTER, Georg Friedrich (II) With wife	America	1817
HOFMEISTER, Gotthilf Imanuel	America	1885
HOFMEISTER, Gottlob Friedrich With family (3 children)	America	1883
HOFMEISTER, Jakob [See S&H 2:156]	America	1803
HOFMEISTER, Jakob (II)	America	1826
HOFMEISTER, Jakob (III)	America	1850
HOFMEISTER, Johann Brother of Christian HOFMEISTER	America	1818

HOFMEISTER, Johann (II)	America	1832
HOFMEISTER, Johannes (I)	Prussian Poland	1803
HOFMEISTER, Johannes (II)	America	1806
HOFMEISTER, Johannes (III) Brother of Balthes Friedrich HOFMEISTER	America	1865
HOFMEISTER, Karl Friedrich	America	1885
HOFMEISTER, Michael, winegrower With family (6 children)	America	1832
HOFMEISTER, Philipp Jakob, winegrower With family (5 children)	America	1852
HOFMEISTER, Simon Gottlob, winegrower	Russia	1879
HOLZER, Julius Went to Montevideo, 1926	Buenos Aires	1929
HONIG, Johann Georg	Prussian Pomerania	1750
HUEBNER, Willi	Philadelphia	1927
HUMMEL, Adolf	Switzerland	1913
HUMMEL, Christiane Philippine	America	1857
HUMMEL, Gottfried Brother of Karl Friedrich HUMMEL	America	1880
HUMMEL, Johann Jakob, winegrower With family (3 children)	America	1817
HUMMEL, Karl Friedrich Brother of Gottfried HUMMEL	America	1880
HUMMEL, Katharine Barbara	America	1857
HUMMEL, Sophie	America	1900

IDLER, Agathe Sister of Margarete and Maria Magdalena IDLER	America	1848
IDLER, Andreas Wilhelm, winegrower With family (2 children)	America	1877
IDLER, Christian Friedrich Ninth child in his family; brother of Johann Jakob and Karl Friedrich IDLER	America	1854
IDLER, Christiane Wilhelmine With her child	America	1843
IDLER, Elisabeth Magdalena	America	1843
IDLER, Gotthilf Daniel	America	1879
IDLER, Gottlob Wilhelm With family (1 child)	America	1879
IDLER, Jakob, winegrower	America	1816
IDLER, Jakob Friedrich	America	1878
IDLER, Johann Jakob Eight child in his family; brother of Christian Friedrich and Karl Friedrich IDLER	America	1854
IDLER, Johann Michael, winegrower With family (4 children)	America	1819
IDLER, Karl Friedrich Fourteenth child in his family; brother of Johann Jakob and Christian Friedrich IDLER	America	1854
IDLER, Karl Ludwig, winegrower With family (3 children)	America	1881
IDLER, Margarete Sister of Agathe and Maria Magdalena IDLER	America	1848
IDLER, Maria Magdalena Sister of Agathe and Margarete IDLER	America	1848
IDLER, Tobias Ferdinand	America	1816
IRION, Christian Gottlieb	America	1867

IRLBECK, Amalie, nee SCHOELLBORN	Palestine	1881

KAESER, --. *See* KUEHNER, --, nee KAESER

KENNER, Albert, mechanic With wife and brother Eugen KENNER	Spain	1921-22
KENNER, Eugen, mechanic With brother Albert KENNER	Spain	1921-22
KEPPLER, Wilhelm Friedrich Ferdinand	America	1869
KIEFHABER, Johannes	America	1810
KIEFHABER, Johannes (II) With mother	America	1828
KIEFHABER, Katharina	America	1805
KIEFHABER, -- With son Johannes KIEFHABER	America	1828
KIENZLEN, Elias	Prussian Pomerania	1750
KIENZLEN, Sybille	Prussian Pomerania	1750
KOCH, Elise	America	1923
KOCH, Karl Ferdinand	America	1869

KOEGEL, Emma. *See* STAENGLE, Emma, nee KOEGEL

KOEGEL, Johannes	Switzerland	1900
KOEGEL, Karl Friedrich, glazier	Switzerland	1880
KOEGEL, Marie Pauline	America	1900
KOEGEL, Richard	America	1900
KOEGEL, Wilhelmine Friedrike	America	1860

KOELZ, Berta	Italy	1890
KOENIG, Johanne Frriedrike, nee MAIER Widow	America	1852
KOENIG, Johannes [*See* S&H 2:169]	America	1805
KOENIG, Karl	America	1880
KOHLER, Elsa. *See* O. FRITZ		
KOHLER, Eugen	America	1923-24
KOHLER, Frida Returned to Nuernberg	Argentina	1921
KOHLER, Luise Christine	America	1854
KOHLER, Otto, machinist [*Dreher*] Died in Fellbach	Argentina	1921
KOHLER, Robert With family (1 child); brother of Eugen and Elsa KOHLER	America	1923-24
KRAFT, Christian Hermann	America	1848
KRAFT, Gottlob David	Switzerland	1849
KRAFT, Johann With wife	Switzerland	1853
KRAFT, Luise Wilhelmine	Switzerland	1854
KRAUTSCHERB, Johannes	Prussian Pomerania	1750
KRESS, Karl	Baltimore	1922
KUEHNER, Karl G.	Holyoke, USA	1924
KUEHNER, Otto With wife, who was -- KUEHNER nee KAESER	Easton, USA	1927

KUENKELE, Christiane   America   1923-26
   Mother of Erwin KUENKELE and Emma MATTHES nee KUENKELE

KUENKELE, Emma. *See* Emma MATTHES nee KUENKELE

KUENKELE, Erwin   America   1923-26
   Son of Christiane KUENKELE; brother of Emma MATTHES :

KUHNLE, Anna Magdalena	Switzerland	1908
KUHNLE, Daniel, winegrower	America	1838
KUHNLE, Dorothea Katharina	America	1853
KUHNLE, Imanuel Gottlob	America	1865
KUHNLE, Jakob, plumber	Switzerland	1908
KUHNLE, Johann Christoph, winegrower With family (2 children)	America	1853
KUHNLE, Johannes	America	1857
KUHNLE, Karl Friedrich	America	1854
KUHNLE, Karl Paulus	Switzerland	1908

LAIBLEN. *Variation of* LAIPPLE

LAIGLE, Georg Friedrich, winegrower With family (3 children)	America	1879
LAIGLE, Jakob	America	1848
LAIGLE, Karl Friedrich, winegrower	America?	1861
LAIGLE, Karoline Friedrike	America	1879
LAIGLE, Marie Pauline	America	1889
LAIGLE, Ulrich Friedrich	America	1819
LAIPPLE, Berta, office worker	America	1923
LAIPPLE, Emma	Argentina	1922

LAIPPLE, Georg Friedrich, winegrower With family (3 children)	America	1879
LAIPPLE, Jakob	America	1848
LAIPPLE, Johann Gottlob With wife	America	1880
LAIPPLE, Johann Gottlob With family (5 children)	America	1879
LAIPPLE, Johann Michael	America	1805
LAIPPLE, Karl Friedrich, winegrower With wife	America	1881
LAIPPLE, Paulus	America	1854
LAIPPLE, Ulrich Friedrich, winegrower	America	1810
LANG, Fritz With family (5 children)	North America	1926
LANG, Hermann Son of Fritz LANG; with wife Margarete LANG nee RADITSCHNIG	America	1927
LANG, Margarete nee RADITSCHNIG With husband Hermann LANG	America	1927
LAUBENGAIER, Hans David	Prussian Pomerania	1750
LEGER, Johann Georg	Prussian Pomerania	1750
LEIBSLE, Christoph Clemens Brother of Ludwig LEIBSLE	America	1850
LEIBSLE, Ludwig Brother of Christoph Clemens LEIBSLE	America	1850
LEINS, Berta nee SCHWINGER With husband Gotthard LEINS and 1 child	Philadelphia	1926
LEINS, Gotthard With wife Berta LEINS nee SCHWINGER and 1 child	Philadelphia	1927

LIPP, Balthes	America	1816
LIPP, Christian Friedrich	Switzerland	1838
LIPP, Emilie	Brazil	1923
LIPP, Georg Michael, winegrower With family (5 children) but without wife	America	1830
LIPP Gottlob, mason With family (8 children)	America	1832
LIPP, Jakob [*See* S&H 2:179, where shown accompanied by three persons]	America	1805
LIPP, Jakob Friedrich	Brazil	1885
LIPP, Jakobine	America	1830
LIPP, Johann Jakob With family (4 children)	America	1854
LIPP, Johannes (I)	Prussian Pomerania	1750
LIPP, Johannes (II)	America	1832
LIPP, Johannes (III)	Switzerland	1838
LIPP, Johannes (IV) With family (1 child)	America	1853
LIPP, Joseph, mason With family (4 children)	America	1853
LIPP, Joseph Friedrich, mason With family (3 children)	America	1857
LIPP, Luise Friedrike	America	1853
LIPP, Wilhelm Friedrich	America	1856
LORENZ, Albert, barber	Switzerland	1900
LORENZ, Georg Wilhelm	America	1857
LORENZ, Gottlob	America	?

LORENZ, Johann Caspar [*See* S&H 2:130, which lists with wife and 3 children]	America	1803
LORENZ, Johann Gottlieb	America	1890
LORENZ, Philipp, winegrower With family (? children)	Russia	1830
LORENZ, Wilhelm Friedrich, winegrower With family (? children)	America	1857
LORENZ, Wilhelm Simon	America	1817
LUZ, August Brother of Gotthilf LUZ	Switzerland	1890
LUZ, Gotthilf Brother of August LUZ	Switzerland	1890
MACK, Ernst With family (1 child); brother of Hans MACK	New York	1927–30
MACK, Hans Brother of Ernst MACK	Chicago	1927–30
MACK, Johann Friedrich, blacksmith Widower with 2 children	America	1852
MAIER, Georg Michael, machinist [*Dreher*] Went to the Province of Georgia [Caucasus]	Russia	1819
MAIER, Johanne Friedrike. *See* Johanne Friedrike KOENIG nee MAIER		
MAILE, Abraham, winegrower With family (5 children)	America	1832
MAILE, Christiane Friedrike	America	1865
MAILE, Georg, laborer Son of Georg MAILE [Senior]	Argentina	1919
MAILE, Gottlob Friedrich, cabinetmaker With family (7 children)	America	1879
MAILE, Hermann	America	1887

MAILE, Jakob Friedrich Brother of Johann Philipp MAILE	America	1856-57
MAILE, Johann	America	1880
MAILE, Johann Philipp Brother of Jakob Friedrich MAILE	America	1856-57
MAILE, Johannes, winegrower With family (6 children)	America	1832
MAILE, Karoline Heinrike	America	1854

MAILE, Matheus Friedrich
    [*But see* S&H 2:171 in which he and his family (6 children)
    are shown as immigrating to Philadelphia in 1805]
	Russia	1804

MAILE, Wilhelm Jakob	America	1881
MANDEL, Ernst Wilhelm	America	1880
MANDEL, Jakob Friedrich, winegrower	Russia	1804
MANDEL, Johannes, coppersmith	France	1845
MATTHES, Elise	America	1928
MATTHES, Emma, nee KUENKELE With husband H. MATTHES and 1 child	America	1923-26
MAYER, Christoph Ernst With sister Luise Friedrike MAYER	America	1879
MAYER, Luise Friedrike With brother Christoph Ernst MAYER	America	1879
MERGENTHALER, Jakob	America	1817
MERGENTHALER, Philipp Heinrich, winegrower With family (2 children)	America	1883

MESSER, Michael
    With family (1 child); returned to Germany in 1858 and was
    in Stuttgart in 1862
	America	1851

MEZGER, Gottlieb Adam With family (7 children)	America	1853
MEZGER, Hermann Ludwig	America	1880
MEZGER, Jakob Friedrich	America	1848
MOHL, Jakob Friedrich, shoemaker	Switzerland	1870
MOHL, Johann Heinrich, mechanic	America	1870
MOSER, Eugen Brother of Hermann MOSER	North America	1922-29
MOSER, Hermann Brother of Eugen MOSER	North America	1922-29
MUELLER, Johann Michael	Russia	1804
MUNDER, Friedrich Karl Johann	America	1846
MUNDER, Karl Gottlob	America	1846
NEEF, August Friedrich, blacksmith	Bohemia	1870
NEEF, Berta	America	1870-85
NEEF, Christiane Luise Sister of Pauline Dorothea NEEF	America	1870
NEEF, Christoph Friedrich [See S&H 2:171, where also spelled NEFF]	America	1805
NEEF, Emilie	America	1870-85
NEEF, Ernst	America	1886
NEEF, Friedrike With 2 children	America	1854
NEEF, Jakob Friedrich (I)	America	1816
NEEF, Jakob Friedrich (II)	America	1838

NEEF, Johann Friedrich, wagon master With family (2 children)	America	1846
NEEF, Karl Heinrich	Bohemia	1870
NEEF, Marie Dorothea Sister of Christopher Friedrich and Jakob Friedrich NEEF	France	1826
NEEF, Pauline Dorothea Sister of Christiane Luise NEEF	America	1870
NEEF, Theodor	America	1870-85
NEEF, Wilhelm Albert	Bohemia	1870
NEEF, Wilhelm Friedrich	America	1853
NOETLING, Karl Christian Ernst, businessman With family (2 children)	America	1854
NOLLENBERGER, Karoline Christine	America	1889
OESTERLE, Christoph Friedrich	America	1810
OESTERLE, Jakob Friedrich, blacksmith With family (8 children)	America	1832
OFF, Johann Caspar, winegrower With family (3 children)	America	1853
OFF, Pauline Sophie	America	1870
OFF, Wilhelm Johann, pilemaker [Feilenhauer]	Switzerland	1870
OTT, Christoph Friedrich With sister Friedrike Rebekka OTT	America	1830
OTT, Friedrike Rebekka With brother Christoph Friedrich OTT	America	1830
OTT, Johann Friedrich, winegrower With family (6 children)	America	1828

OTT, Johann Friedrich (II), mason With family (5 children)	America	1854
OTT, Johann Philipp Died in Philadelphia in 1836	America	1833
OTT, Johannes	America	1852
OTT, Karl Wilhelm, winegrower	America	1879
OTT, Karl Wilhelm (II)	Argentina	1921
OTT, Michael, winegrower With family (8 children)	America	1853
OTTENBACHER, Johann Jakob	America	1881
OTTENBACHER, Marie Luise	Paris, France	1860
OTTENBACHER, Wilhelm, day laborer Returned to Germany in 1890	America	1888
PAULUS, Jonathan	Palestine	1875
PAULUS, Philipp	Switzerland	1866
PFANDER, Barbara Widow of winegrower; with 5 children	America	1854

PFANDER, Elisabetha Katharina
  Sister of Philipp, Johann Christoph, Johannes, and Euphrosine
  PFANDER
	America	1831

PFANDER, Euphrosine
  Sister of Philipp, Johann Christoph, Elisabeth Katharina,
  and Johannes PFANDER
	America	1832

PFANDER, Georg David, winegrower With family (? children)	America	1853
PFANDER, Gottlieb Brother of Karl and Wilhelm PFANDER	America	1880
PFANDER, Gottlob Friedrich	America	1865
PFANDER, Jakob Friedrich	America	1854

PFANDER, Johann Christoph Brother of Philipp, Elisabeth Katharina, Johannes, and Euphrosine PFANDER	America	1830
PFANDER, Johann Michael	America	1852
PFANDER, Johannes, winegrower Brother of Philipp, Johann Christoph, Elisabeth Katharina, and Euphrosine PFANDER; emigrated with family (3 children)	Russia	1832
PFANDER, Johannes (II)	Russia	1880
PFANDER, Karl Brother of Gottlieb and Wilhelm PFANDER	America	1880
PFANDER, Karl Heinrich	America	1854
PFANDER, Philipp Brother of Johann Christoph, Elisabeth Katharina, Johannes, and Euphrosine PFANDER	America	1815
PFANDER, Philipp (II)	America	1838
PFANDER, Wilhelm Brother of Karl and Gottlieb PFANDER	America	1880
PFEIL, Wilhelm Friedrich, tailor	America	1844
PFUND, Georg Friedrich, winegrower With family (3 children)	America	1854
PLOSS, Johannes	America	1831
PLOSS. *See also* BLOSS		
PRIESTER, Bernhard With wife Klara Priester nee WISSMANN	America	1928
PRIESTER, Emma	North America	1927
PRIESTER, Klara, nee WISSMANN With husband Bernhard PRIESTER	America	1928

RADITSCHNIG, Konrad Brother of Margarete LANG nee RADITSCHNIG	North America	1930

RADITSCHNIG, Margarete. *See* Margarete LANG nee RADITSCHNIG

RAISCH, Christiane
   Sister of Friedrich and Gottlieb RAISCH; [*see* S&H 2:188, where
   listed as Christian RAISCH]
	America	1805

RAISCH, Friedrich
   Brother of Christiane and Gottlieb RAISCH; [not listed in
   S&H with sibling immigrants]
	America	1805

RAISCH, Gottlieb
   Brother of Christiane and Friedrich RAISCH; [*see* S&H 2:188,
   where listed as Goodly RAISCH]
	America	1805

RAISCH, Gottlieb (II) [Not listed in S&H and might refer to Gottlieb (I) RAISCH]	America	1806
RAISCH, Gottlob Wilhelm, winegrower With family (9 children)	America	1880
RAISCH, Jakobine	America	1866
RAISCH, Johann, beer brewer With family (6 children)	America	1880
RAISCH, Johannes	America	1805
RAISCH, Karl, engineer	America	1920
RAISER, Alwine Sister of Martha and Theodor RAISER	North America	19-?
RAISER, Martha Sister of Alwine and Theodor RAISER	North America	19-?
RAISER, Theodor Brother of Martha and Alwine RAISER	North America	19-?
RAPP, Eugen Brother of Willy RAPP	North America	1923
RAPP, Michael	Prussian Pomerania	1750

RAPP, Willy   North America   1923
    Brother of Eugen RAPP

REBMANN, Christian Friedrich   America   1853

REBMANN, Georg David   Prussian Pomerania 1750

REBMANN, Gottlob Friedrich, winegrower   America   1880
    With family (5 children)

REBMANN, Jakob Friedrich, winegrower   America   1865

REBMANN, Johann, winegrower   America   1854
    Widower

REBMANN, Johann Friedrich, winegrower   America   1829

REBMANN, Johann Friedrich (II), winegrower America   1852

REBMANN, Johann Georg, winegrower   America   1820
    With family (5 children)

REBMANN, Johann Michael   America   1816

REBMANN, Johannes, winegrower   America   1852
    With wife

REBMANN, Johannes (II), winegrower   America   1852
    With family (3 children)

REBMANN, Karl Gottlob, [picture] painter   Switzerland   1888

REBMANN, Katharine Wilhelmine   America   1852

REBMANN, Philipp Jakob, winegrower   Russia   1829
    With family (8 children); "living until now [1934?] in
    Gnadental, of. Areis, Jud. Cet. Alba, Rumania"

REBMANN, Philipp Jakob   Switzerland   1897

REBMANN, Simon   America   1806
    [See S&H 2:189, where listed with thirteen member family]

REHART, Hermann   Sweden   1931
    With wife

REICK, Gottfried   America   1849

34

REICK, Jakob	America	1848
REICK, Johann Friedrich	America	1846
REICK, Michael Friedrich	America	1849
REICK, Michael Friedrich (II)	America	1870
REICK, Philipp David, winegrower With family (1 child)	America	1853
REUCHLEN, Mattheus With family (? children)	America	1817
RIEGER, August Friedrich	America	1883
RIEGER, Ernst, mechanic	Argentina	1921
RIEGER, Michael Gottlob	America	1854
RIEHLE, Richard Returned to Germany	Argentina	1921
RIENTH, Ernst	Switzerland	1910
RIENTH, Hermann His wife and 2 children followed him to America in 1925.	America	1923
ROEHM, Emilie	North America	1927
ROMMEL, Gottlob Friedrich	Switzerland	1904
ROMMEL, Philipp Friedrich	America	1854
ROMMEL, Wilhelm Friedrich Brother of Philipp Friedrich ROMMEL	America	1865
ROSIN, Johann Philipp With family (8 children)	Russia (Caucasus)	1819
RUBE, Christiane Philippine	France	1869

RUBE, Marie	America	1884
RUOFF, Johann Friedrich With family (? children)	America	1817
RUOFF, Ulrich, Junior	America	1817
SAILER, Agathe With her child	America	1817
SAILER, Friedrich	Prussian Pomerania	1800
SAILER, Johann Heinrich	America	1886
SAILER, Johann Jakob With family (3 children)	America	1885
SAILER, Johann Philipp	America	1816

SAILER, Johann Thomas
  With sister Katharina; [*See* S&H s:168 which lists Thomas and
  Barbara SILER]
	America	1805

SAILER, Johannes "Said to be in America"	America	1830
SAILER, Johannes (II) With family (2 children)	America	1883
SAILER, Johannes (III) Brother of Karl Friedrich SAILER	America	1885
SAILER, Jost	Prussian Pomerania	1800
SAILER, Karl Friedrich Brother of Johannes (III) SAILER	America	1885
SAILER, Katharina With brother Johann Thomas SAILER	America	1805
SAILER, Philipp Friedrich, carpenter With family (6 children)	America	1881
SAILER, Simon	Switzerland	1886
SAILER, Thomas	Prussian Pomerania	1750

SAILER, Wilhelm	Spain	1921
SAILER, Wilhelm Michael	Russia	1804
SCHAECHTERLE, Agate	America	1819
SCHAECHTERLE, Albert Later returned to Germany, where he died.	America	1922
SCHAECHTERLE, Gottfried	America	1847
SCHAECHTERLE, Gottlieb	America	1832
SCHAECHTERLE, Johann Philipp	America	1816
SCHAECHTERLE, Johannes, butcher With family (2 children)	America	1854
SCHAECHTERLE, Luise	America	1870
SCHAECHTERLE, Margaretha Barbara	America	1819
SCHAECHTERLE, Margarethe Luise	America	1832
SCHAECHTERLE, Otto	America	1930
SCHAECHTERLE, Paulus	America	1834
SCHAECHTERLE, Philipp Jakob With wife	America	1883
SCHAEFER, Gustav Brother of Robert SCHAEFER	St. Louis, USA	1923
SCHAEFER, Joseph Friedrich, winegrower With family (5 children)	America	1819
SCHAEFER, Karoline	North America	1927
SCHAEFER, Michael Ludwig	America	1866
SCHAEFER, Paul	Switzerland	1900
SCHAEFER, Robert Brother of Gustav SCHAEFER	St. Louis, USA	1923

SCHAIBLE, Hedwig. *See* STIERLE, Hedwig nee SCHAIBLE

SCHAIBLE, Martha   America   1927-28
    With sister Hedwig STIERLE nee SCHAIBLE

SCHECK, Maria   Italy   1923
    Returned to Germany and married W. BURGEL in 1926

SCHEDELEN, Andreas   Prussian Pomerania 1750

SCHEDELEN, Martin   Prussian Pomerania 1750

SCHEURENBRAND, Johannes, shoemaker   America   1885

SCHILLING, Elisabethe Katharine   America   1864

SCHILLING, Johann Philipp   America   1854

SCHILLING, Philipp Friedrich   France   1865

SCHILLING, Wilhelm Gottlob   America   1854

SCHMID, Christian   America   1819

SCHMID, Erwin   America   1923

SCHMID, Georg Friedrich   America   1804
    [Probably the family mentioned in S&H 2:179 (3 persons)]

SCHMID, Heinrike   America   1855
    Sister of Philippine Karoline, Pauline Katharine, and
    Johanna Philippine SCHMID

SCHMID, Johann Ludwig   America   1832

SCHMID, Johanna Philippine   America   1855
    Sister of Philippine Karoline, Pauline Katharine, and
    Heinrike SCHMID

SCHMID, Johannes, winegrower   Russia   1819
    With family (? children)

SCHMID, Julie   America   1923

38

SCHMID, Karl August, saddler	America	1864
SCHMID, Matheus Friedrich [See S&H 2:171, where spelled SCHMIDT]	America	1805
SCHMID, Pauline Katharine Sister of Philippine Katharine, Heinrike, and Johanna Philippine SCHMID	America	1855
SCHMID, Paulus	America	1817
SCHMID, Philippine Karoline Sister of Pauline Katharine, Heinrike, and Johanna Philippine SCHMID	America	1853
SCHMID, Wilhelmine Sister of Paulus Schmid	America	1819
SCHNABEL, Johanna	America	1830
SCHNABEL, Johanna Luise	America	1880

SCHNAITHMANN, Johanna Friedrike. *See* SEIBOLD, Friedrike nee
SCHNAITHMANN

SCHNAITMANN, Anna Dorothea Seventh child in her family; sister of Johannes IV SCHNAITMANN and other siblings herein listed	America	1852
SCHNAITMANN, Anna Maria Ninth child in her family; sister of Johannes (IV) SCHNAITMANN and other siblings herein listed	America	1852
SCHNAITMANN, August Heinrich Brother of Gottlob Friedrich SCHNAITMANN	America	1854
SCHNAITMANN, Christian Friedrich	America	1857
SCHNAITMANN, Christiane Magdalena	America	1854
SCHNAITMANN, Christoph Simon	America	1804
SCHNAITMANN, Eugen, machinist Brother of Karl SCHNAITMANN	North America	1925-26

SCHNAITMANN, Friedrike   America   1852
  Twelfth child in her family; sister of Johannes (IV) SCHNAITMANN
  and other siblings herein listed

SCHNAITMANN, Georg Friedrich Gustav   England   1869
  Businessman

SCHNAITMANN, Gottlob Friedrich   America   1854
  Brother of August Heinrich SCHNAITMANN

SCHNAITMANN, Gottlob Friedrich (II)   America   1857

SCHNAITMANN, Jakob, hired hand   Basel, Switzerland 1890

SCHNAITMANN, Johann Eberhard   France   1788

SCHNAITMANN, Johann Friedrich   America   1852
  Sixth child in his family; brother of Johannes (IV) SCHNAITMANN
  and other siblings herein listed

SCHNAITMANN, Johann Jakob   America   1884

SCHNAITMANN, Johanne Christiane   America   1854

SCHNAITMANN, Johanne Friedrike   America   1880

SCHNAITMANN, Johannes (I)   Russia   1809

SCHNAITMANN, Johannes (II), winegrower   America   1830
  With family (2 children)

SCHNAITMANN, Johannes (III)   America   1852

SCHNAITMANN, Johannes (IV)   America   1852
  Second child in his family; brother of Anna Dorothea, Anna
  Maria, Friedrike, and Johann Friedrich SCHNAITMANN

SCHNAITMANN, Johannes (V)   America   1854

SCHNAITMANN, Johannes (VI)   America   1873
  Brother of Wilhelm Friedrich Gustav SCHNAITMANN

SCHNAITMANN, Joseph   America   1832
  Said to have returned to Germany

SCHNAITMANN, Karl, auto mechanic   America   1925-26
  Brother of Eugen SCHNAITMANN

SCHNAITMANN, Karl   North America   1901

SCHNAITMANN, Luise	America	1830

Eleventh child in her family; sister of Johannes (IV) SCHNAITMANN
and other siblings herein listed

SCHNAITMANN, Magdalena	America	1854

Widow with 5 children

SCHNAITMANN, Maria	America	1880

SCHNAITMANN, Maria Barbara	America	1854

SCHNAITMANN, Mathilde	America	1880

SCHNAITMANN, Mattheus Friedrich, winegrower	America	1844

With family (3 children)

SCHNAITMANN, Michael	Prussian Pomerania	1750

SCHNAITMANN, Paul	California	1920

SCHNAITMANN, Philipp Friedrich, winegrower	Russia	1879

With family (3 children); returned to Germany

SCHNAITMANN, Robert, businessman	Switzerland	1914

SCHNAITMANN, Wilhelm Friedrich, winegrower	America	1869

SCHNEIDER, Gottfried Ernst	America	1804

SCHNELLER, Johanna, nee ALLEMNDINGER	Jerusalem	1887

Wife of Ludwig Theodor SCHNELLER; went to the Syrian orphanage

SCHOELLHORN, Amalie	Palestine	1891

Returned in 1896 and married -- IRLBECK, [picture] painter

SCHOELLHORN, Anna Magdalena	Americz	1852

With her child

SCHOELLHORN, Dorothea	America	1849

SCHOELLHORN, Gottlieb Friedrich	America	1832

Cabinetmaker; with family (1 child)

SCHOELLHORN, Johann Georg	America	1831

SCHOELLHORN, Johannes, cabinetmaker	Switzerland	1882
SCHOELLHORN, Karl Gotthilf, weaver With family (2 children)	America	1882
SCHOELLHORN, Karoline Luise	America	1867
SCHOELLHORN, Katharina Barbara	America	1852
SCHOELLHORN, Katharina Magdalena	America	1867
SCHOELLHORN, Philippine	America	1852
SCHOELLHORN, Sophie With her 2 children	America	1853
SCHREINER, Gottlob, missionary	South Africa	1854
SCHREINER, Katharina	America	1854
SCHREINER, Philipp	Prussian Pomerania	1750
SCHRIEB, Christian Friedrich, winegrower With family (6 children)	America	1866
SCHRIEB, Christiane Karoline	America	1853
SCHRIEB, Georg Johannes	America	1830
SCHRIEB, Wilhelm Jakob, winegrower	America	1830
SCHUER, Gottlob, winegrower	America	1848
SCHUH, Friedrich	Philadelphia	1927
SCHUNTER, Otto	Detroit	1925
SCHURR, Jakob	Hungary	1818
SCHURR, Johann Jakob, blacksmith	Hungary	1800
SCHWAB, Katharina Charlotte	America	1853

SCHWARZ, Karl, cabinetmaker With wife	Argentina	1920
SCHWARZ, Karl (II) With family (6 children); returned to Germany in 1927	Greece	1924
SCHWILKE, Dorothea Widow with 8 children	America	1849
SCHWILKE, Euphrosina Sister of Johannes SCHWILKE	America	1817
SCHWILKE, Jakob, winegrower With family (3 children)	America	1878
SCHWILKE, Johannes Brother of Euphrosina SCHWILKE	America	1817
SCHWILKE, Johannes (II)	America	1878
SCHWILKE, Karl Friedrich, winegrower With family (3 children)	America	1828
SCHWILKE, Philippine	America	1878
SCHWINGER, Berta. *See* LEINS, Berta nee SCHWINGER		
SEEGER, Johann Philipp	Prussian Poland	1803
SEEMUELLER, Abraham	America	1835
SEEMUELLER, Johann Friedrich	America	1852
SEEMUELLER, Johanna Luise	America	1857
SEEMUELLER, Johannes, tailor With family (6 children)	America	1844
SEEMUELLER, Luise Friedrike With her child; sister of of Johann Friedrich SEEMUELLER	America	1854
SEEMUELLER, Mattheus Friedrich With family (? children); [*see* S&H 2:166, wherein 4 children]	America	1805

SEEMUELLER, Philip Jakob, winegrower   America   1816
   With family (6 children); brother of Mattheus Friedrich SEE-
MUELLER

SEIBOLD, Adolf. *See* SEYBOLD, Adolf

SEIBOLD, Balthas, farmer   America   1854
   With family (7 children)

SEIBOLD, Christian Jakob   America   1883
   With family (2 children)

SEIBOLD, Emma   North America   1928
   Sister of Karl SEIBOLD

SEIBOLD, Ernst   North America   1920

SEIBOLD, Ernst (II)   Argentina   1921

SEIBOLD, Euphrosine, nee HAEUSSERMANN   America   1855
   Widow with 3 children

SEIBOLD, Eugen   North America   1922

SEIBOLD, Georg Michael   America   1835

SEIBOLD, Gotthif   America   1883

SEIBOLD, Gottlieb   America   1830

SEIBOLD, Gottlieb Friedrich, winegrower   America   1880
   With family (1 child)

SEIBOLD, Gottlob   America   1893

SEIBOLD, Hermann   Argentina   1921

SEIBOLD, Johann Friedrich   America   1854
   Widower with 2 children

SEIBOLD, Johann Jakob   America   1849

SEIBOLD, Johanna Friedrike, nee SCHNAITHMANN America   1830
   Widow with 7 children

SEIBOLD, Johannes, shoemaker   America   1832
   Widower with 4 children

SEIBOLD, Johannes (II)	America	1853
SEIBOLD, Johannes (III), winegrower	America	1883
SEIBOLD, Karl, missionary Missionary in Foulat Islands	Basel, Switzerland	1912
SEIBOLD, Karl (II), winegrower	Argentina	1921
SEIBOLD, Katharina Barbara With her son	America	1856
SEIBOLD, Luise Christiane	America	1854
SEIBOLD, Luise Friedrike	America	1854
SEIBOLD, Maria	America	1913
SEIBOLD, Michael, shoemaker With wife	America	1835
SEIBOLD, Sophie Margarethe	America	1831
SEIBOLD, Wilhelm Friedrich	America	1855
SEIBOLD, Wilhelm Gottlob	America	1856
SEYBOLD, Adolf With wife and 1 child	North America	1929
SIEGEL, Ludwig Friedrich	Brazil	1900
SIMON, Eugen	North America	1923
SIMON, Jakob	North America	1817
STAEHLE, Johann Jakob, cabinetmaker With family (3 children)	America	1854
STAENGLE, Emma, nee KOEGEL With husband Karl STAENGLE and 1 child	New York	1927
STAENGLE, Karl With wife Emma STAENGLE, nee KOEGEL, and 1 child	New York	1927

STAHL, Franz Jakob	America	1850
STIERLE, A. With wife Hedwig STIERLE, nee SCHAIBLE	America	1927-28
STIERLE, Hedwig, nee SCHAIBLE With husband A. Stierle and sister Martha SCHAIBLE	America	1927-28
STILZ, Fritz Returned to Germany	Argentina	1922
STOLL, Anna Elisabethe	America	1819
STOLL, Anna Maria	Poland	1800
STOLL, Ferdinand, blacksmith	Switzerland	1880
STOLL, Gottlieb	America	1865
STOLL, Johann Jakob	America	1819
STOLL, Johannes	America	1824
STOLL, Johannes (II)	America	1857
STOLL, Karl Friedrich, blacksmith	Switzerland	1850
STOLL, Pauline	Switzerland	1867
STOLL, Willy	North America	1927
STOLZ, Gustav Returned to Germany	Argentina	1922
TRABER, Emil Brother of Paul TRABER	North America	1923-27
TRABER, Paul Brother of Emil TRABER	North America	1923-27

VAIHINGER, Josua, winegrower
   With family (4? children); emigrated for religious reasons;
   [see S&H 2:155, wherein 7 children][also see Introduction]
	America	1804

VOGT, Johannes, winegrower	America	1837
VOGT, Philipp Jakob With family (4 children)	America	1816
VOTTELER, Gustav Brother of Klara VOTTELER	North America	1921-27
VOTTELER, Klara Sister of Gustav VOTTELER	North America	1921-27
WACKENHUT, Hermann Returned to Germany	Argentina	1921
WAGNER, Elisabeth Barbara	America	1829
WAGNER, Friedrike With 3 children	America	1852
WAGNER, Georg Friedrich [See S&H 2:165, wherein wife and 2 children are listed]	America	1805
WAGNER, Gotthold	America	1929
WAGNER, Johann Jakob, winegrower	America	1810
WAGNER, Michael Friedrich	France	1810
WAHL, Christian Konrad, winegrower	America	1817
WAHL, Katharina	America	1817
WALTER, Johann Friedrich, winegrower Widower with 6 children	America	1819
WALTER, Johann Philipp, winegrower With family (7 children)	America	1831
WEBER, Alois, cabinetmaker	Switzerland	1908
WEBER, Christoph Eberhard	America	1857
WEBER, Lina Returned to Germany	Argentina	1924

WESSNER, Christina Frederika. *See* KOENIG, Christina Frederika, nee WESSNER

WIDMANN, Eugen Brother of Klara WIDMANN	America	1923-27
WIDMANN, Klara Sister of Eugen WIDMANN	America	1923-27

WISSMANN, Klara. *See* PRIESTER, Klara, nee WISSMANN

WOEHRLE, Eugen	America	1927
WOELFLE, Euphrosina	America	1806

WOELFLE, --
    Three unmarried brothers; *see* S&H 2:165, wherein a
    Georg WOELFLE (spelled WOLFLEY) is listed together
    with the WAGNER and ZERWICK families, also in this
    monograph]
	America	1805

WOELLHAF, Georg Jakob, shoemaker	Switzerland	1804
WOERNER, Georg	Prussian Pomerania	1750
WUENSCH, Johanna Luise	America	1817
ZENDEL, Adolf	America	1905
ZENDEL, Ernst	Hungary	1910

ZERWECK, Christian
    [*see* S&H 2:165, which shows him arriving at Philadelphia
    in 1805]
	America	1810

ZERWECK, Georg Daniel	America	1810
ZERWECK, Gottlob Friedrich	America	1863
ZERWECK, Johann Michael	America	1810

ZERWECK, Wilhelm Friedrich, baker With family (1 child)	America	1881
ZERWECK, Wilhelm Gottlob	America	1881
ZIMMERMANN, Karl, plumber	America	1867

www.ingramcontent.com/pod-product-compliance
Lightning Source LLC
Chambersburg PA
CBHW081204270326
41930CB00014B/3292